Reflections of Light

by David Jamison

Second Edition

ISBN 978-1-949432-10-7

Published by:

Inner Alchemy's Publishing (Inner Alchemy's)
332 S. Michigan Ave.
Ste 121-C141
Chicago, IL 60604-4434

info@inneralchemys.com
www.inneralchemys.com

Printed in the United States of America

Contents

Acknowledgements

David Morris Jamison's book of poetry and verses is not only a reflection of his personal experiences and passions, but also an inspiration for those who seek to make a difference in the world and appreciate the beauty of life. Whether you are looking for guidance, solace, or simply to be entertained, this book is a must-read for those who appreciate thought-provoking and highly inspirational poetry.

My special thanks to Tony Vortex of the MetaCenterChicago.com metaphysical organization in Chicago, and my MetaCenter family, who have given me the support, empowerment, and encouragement to revise and re-release my first published collection of poetry and verse, originally released to a small group of family and friends in 2004!

I further continue to dedicate this book, and any future books, that I may create...to the memory of my parents King D. & Maggie L. Jamison, along with my daughter Devin, and my son Yusef & (Liana), in addition to my three wonderful grandchildren, Dawn, Sean, and Joaquin.

And my most gracious humble acknowledgement goes to "The Creator of All Things...First Prime Creator" for writing this work...and all that may follow...through its vessel...called David.

Foreword

God" beyond your highest concept" is in these pages...just as God "beyond your highest concept" is in the hands holding these pages.

I offer you blessings for your highest & best to support & empower your life experience on this earth!

You already have your own contract/blueprint laid out for your life... may you stay true to it's purpose. You already have your own Guardian Angel assigned to you, to support and empower you whenever called upon, or waiver from your purpose. You already have other Spiritual guides, and Teachers awaiting you to call upon them. Whether it's a frantic thought of "I need help" or a verbal request they will, and do respond.

I salute the "Spiritual Hero" within you... within these pages a remembrance will come upon thee...that you and I are, to quote my dear friend Rev. Michael Beckwith, "Simply here for God!"

Higher Love and Light,
David Morris Jamison

A Timeless Message from Three Wise "Ones"

Marianne Williamson

Jalal ad-din Rumi...

Goethe

It is our Light, not our Darkness that frightens us!

Our deepest fear is not that we are inadequate.

Our deepest fear is that we are powerful beyond measure.

It is our light, not our darkness, that frightens us.

We ask ourselves, who am I to be brilliant,
gorgeous, talented and fabulous?

Actually, who are you not to be?

You are a child of God.

Your playing small doesn't serve the world.

There's nothing enlightened about shrinking so that
other people won't feel insecure around you.

We were born to make manifest the glory of God that is within us.

It's not just in some of us, it's in everyone.

And as we let our own light shine, we unconsciously give other
people permission to do the same. As we are liberated from our own
fears, our presence automatically liberates others.

**Marianne Williamson
A Course In Miracles**

The One Thing You Must Do

There is one thing in this world which you must never forget to do. If you forget everything else and not this, there's nothing to worry about, but if you remember everything else and forget this, then you will have done nothing in your life.

It's as if a king has sent you to some country to do a task, and you perform a hundred other services, but not the one he sent you to do. So human beings come to this world to do particular work. That work is the purpose, and each is specific to the person. If you don't do it, it's as though a priceless Indian sword were used to slice rotten meat. It's a golden bowl being used to cook turnips, when one filing from the bowl could buy a hundred suitable pots. It's like a knife of the finest tempering nailed into a wall to hang things on.

You say, "But look, I'm using the dagger. It's not lying idle." Do you hear how ludicrous that sounds? For a penny an iron nail could be bought to serve for that. You say, "But I spend my energies on lofty enterprises. I study jurisprudence and philosophy and logic and astronomy and medicine and all the rest." But consider why you do those things. They are all branches of yourself.

Remember the deep root of your being, the presence of your lord. Give your life to the one who already owns your breath and your moments. If you don't, you will be exactly like the man who takes a precious dagger and hammers it into his kitchen wall for a peg to hold his dipper gourd. You'll be wasting valuable keenness and foolishly ignoring your dignity and your purpose.

Jalal ad-din Rumi
(1207-1273)

Commitment

Until one is committed, there is hesitancy, the chance to draw back, always ineffectiveness. Concerning all acts of initiative and creation there is one elementary truth (the ignorance of which kills countless ideas and splendid plans) that the moment one definitely commits oneself, then Providence moves, too. All sorts of things occur to help one that would never otherwise have occurred. A whole stream of events issues from that decision, raising in one's favor all manner of unforeseen incidents and meetings and material assistance, which no man could have dreamed would have come his way. Whatever you can do, or dream you can, begin it. Boldness has genius, power and magic in it. Begin it now.

Goethe

Unlock Me
(The Peacekeepers Prayer)

God unlock the Peace in my heart...
I release it to the world
God unlock the Love in my heart...
I release it to the world
God unlock the Joy in my heart...
I release it to the world
God unlock me...
Iam the world!

God unite us in our divisions
that I may become One
with my brothers and sisters...
and One with the world!

Hiding

As I am shy
I'm always hiding
I hide in windows
I hide my face in television
I hide my voice on the radio
I hide my heart under my shirt
I hide my breathe in the air
I hide...I'm always hiding
I'm glad God can see me...
Sometimes when I'm afraid
I hide in Him!

Who Killed the Dreamer in You?

The dreamer who danced with you at 2
and laughed with you at 8
who killed
who killed the dreamer in you?

As years passed quickly with forlorn
where are ideas that were higher than the com
where are the dreams that lifted the sun to the mom
where are the why's, how's, and what fors
that were inward born?

Again my beloved
where has the dreamer gone in you
who has killed him...cloaked him...
or cast him aside
open up...open up...
and let again the dreamer arise

For what better vehicle
than to rise again...through your eyes
and shine, and heal, and touch
those close to you now...
those that you love so much!

You are...you are...
this you shall surely say
that in my light of being
I have led you to dream again
in my beloved way

Not by might
not by power
but by my spirit
the dreamer shall always
have its way

Behold...
I awaken the dreamer again in you
to rise and conquer
the deafness and apathy
that has arisen within

My beloved
the dreamer in you is anew
go forth...and make an abundance of
great wishes...and great themes
to fill and beautify your world
with my God spirit
that is always nearer than near to you!

My beloved...
go forth and BE the dream...
for as you shall be in it...
it shall be in you!

My Lords Prayer

My father which art in me
hallowed be thy name
thy kingdom is come...thy will is done
within, as it is done without!
Lord give me this day
bountiful abundance in all my needs
and forgive my debts
as I forgive my debtors
and protect me from temptations
and deliver me from evil
for the Creation behind thee is the kingdom
and the power, and the glory forever...
Thank you my father!

I Am All That Is

I stand in the moment of Creation
I am...I see...I be...
I am the God thee pray to see
Your reflection is me...and I am thee

Man at his best...is a reflection of God
there is no greater truth

Man at his worst...is a reflection of God
there is no greater truth

God is in every man and she-man
simply some realize his presence sooner than others
There is no place God is not
simply some feel his presence sooner than others

God is still God...is still God...is still God
Whether you believe in him (or her) or not!
God is still God...is still God...is still God
Whether you recognize his different costumes
or physical illusions or not!

That what you think you know...isn't
that what you don't know still...is
Just know this...That I am your rock...your only rock
there is nothing else to know!

Don't You Recognize Me?

Who art the man
which standeth on the bedrock
of the earth...
With the canopy of the darkened
heavens above his gaze?

Who art this being of wonderment
who eats...breathes...loves...and
births its young amidst a
radiating stream of life-force
emanating from our earth
mother's womb?

Where from comes this man's
shadow... if light
abides not
from his crown?

Who knoweth this mans name
or what land he hails from?
Perhaps a distinguishing mark
..No none has been seen!

Or perhaps...(this may be a better solution) even if
he
stood before me
without God's eyes...him I still
would not see!
Because looking out and looking
backward...I would not even
recognize Me!!!

A mask of God
is who I be...
be...be...be!

Saying Goodbye To A Dream

Saying goodbye to a dream
is not what it might seem
cause thoughts that caused it
still tend to be weaned
on actions...and perceptions
still strong and lean.

Some have taken shape
others still are in the dream
But the Creator who authored them
has demanded that they show
up to be seen.

Some unrecognizable...some
are clear
But all reflect their authors
face of love so dear
which shields the adversary's
presence of fear!

It matters not
the clothes they wear
for all again simply bear
the resemblance of their author's stare

So blessed one...
Be mindful of the thoughts
you hold...so bold
cause your mind is the Creator's mold
Asking you to author
only that which the Creation...
can lovingly spin into spiritual gold

So thus...hence forth
from thine meditations
you cannot say
you have not been emphatically told!

I Hold On To Everything
By Holding On To Nothing!

I hold on to life
by releasing my sights
until my beloved...! view it all again
in the Light!

Whispering winds
hold not the changes
until the last leaf falls to the
limits of its ranges

A cloudless night
bear all in its stead
until the harvest moon
appears with its
mists of blistering red

A hero's not welcomed
at his home...not ever
till the dawn welcomes his sunset
of his last endeavor

I hold on to light
by embracing my shadow
I hold on to God
by standing still in his window

I hold on to rain
by blessing the ocean
I hold on to hope
by keeping good notions

I hang on to all
everyday in wait
while my brother scowers the landscape
for another way to heaven's gate

I look to some
and I see pity
as I look over my shoulder
while they spiritually starve in the cities

I have everything
yet... I've misplaced my pot
for the fluid in my body
races for relief
at the ist empty spot!

I am a King
but I've lost my horse
now I have to walk among
the people...
an actually hear their discourse!

And sick as I am
as I spend as I might
I still want for love
on this lonely night!

I've give up gain
and I'm strong I'm sure
but lust chases me yet...
So I guess I'm "just" almost pure!

But stand still as I may
because I'm still a selfish man
I've released all...to gain it again...
This time by God's great "hand!"

The Power of Light

What giveth a candle
power over the darkness?
How is it that a flicker of light
can illumine a great cave?
What power possesses it
beyond its size and girth
and does this power within
emanate from within
or without the earth?
The magistrations of God
seeketh to balance all in peace.
That's why He keeps sending lights...
so the ignorance eventually
in man... will cease!

My Mother

My Mother...My Mother
I love so well
little does she know
how great is her loving spell!

Many a time
I've looked at her in awe
as I ponder
the trees of my life
she's cleared...
without aid of a physical saw!

Always a smile...
"Baby, it'll be alright"
my pasts
been a credence
to her prophetic sight!

Or a little bit here...
and a little bit there
and I've found troubles
done past
without my having to give
it my stare!

Don't know what the world
was like... before I came
But since it didn't
give my Mother a medal
it must be ashamed!

Again I don't know
the politics of such!
But my father was
a great man...
and He recognized as much!

So I'll give it to ignorance
of a citywide few
they just didn't recognize her
I'll assume
cause they didn't have
my view!

My Mother...My Mother
I have to say it
again and again
God favors you most
among all the daughters
of men...

However,
for the life of me
I still can't figure out...when
the world will see you
as I see you...
a wonderful heaven and earth blend!

Perhaps it's true...
I'm prejudiced
because I'm the blessed
Son...
Just thought I'd tell
you now...
While we both can hold
hands as one!

I am Everyman

All that I am...is man
All man is...I am
I am the strongest of the strong
of man.

I am the weakest of the weak
of man,
What I am ...
is what I am!

What I am
is my evolution
What you perceive me to be
is your evolution!

The God that I am,
maybe a devil you may see
whatever the image,
Me is what I be!

I dance with the beasts
and float with the doves...
I am He that others
to see face east!
Iam also He that changes
human costumes like gloves...

He that you see
is who you choose
for me to be...
So you can feel
free!

For how can a God's son
be a slave?
What man of angels
brought David's seed from the graves?

Who do you see...
Who do you think I be?

The Princess of Momme

There now lives a little princess
under the age of one...
Who lived with her mother
under the midwestern sun.

Her royalty and beauty
always bring the crowds to glee
for few royal children
was as sweet as she!

Though tiny of height
and foot size small
she ruled over her kingdom
Winter through Fall.

And sometimes difficult
she could be,
But again...only those times
mother would see.

And yet in still
Dawn presides...
from her bedroom
under the royal Minnesota skies

Her toys...she commands
with an iron will
even her Barbie's bow
when her tea she does spill.

So here's a toast
to love and success,
for next year again...she be crowned
Momme's Little Princess!

Little Girls

Little girls are like whispers of frankincense and myrrh
confiding to the Creation's Heaven of the passions they shall stir...

As it's gales of temperament finally subside,
unveiling God's most blessed spectacle...
an image of the birth of Jesus -
in His sky.

From the southern lows
to the northern highs...
The clouds cry and spill their dew
over the small crowd of witnesses so few.

But alas, none care to cover
cause they all desire to see...
the Mother of one
who brought thee to me!

Our little girls are all
growing to be
the fragrance of our lives
who deliver the treasures of the earth
that the Angelic host can plainly see

So when next you get the scent
of frankincense and myrrh,
cast thine eyes to the heavens
and witness God and His Angels concur...
So be it!

Family

A million families
a million dreams
a million infants
a million teens

Dad and moms are beaming bright
about their families still holding tight
Lamps are lit at evenings fade
remembering the vows again they made.

Son are strong
with confidence of limb
and daughters ponder
their latest shopping whim

Bills lay flat on the dresser draw
as dad sweats heavily
over the interest due
by law!

But as a family
there is no threat...
because the Million family march
hedged their bet!

Who Are You?

Who are the man
which standeth on the bedrock of the earth...
with the canopy of the arkened
heavens above his gaze?

Who art this being of wonderment
who eats...breathes...loves...
and births its young
amidst a radiating stream of life-force
emanating from our earth
mother's womb?

Where from comes this man's shadow
if light
abides not
from his crown?

Who knoweth this man's name
or what land he hails
Perhaps a distinguishing mark...
no none has been seen!

Or perhaps,
even if he stood before me
without God's eyes
he... would not see!

Because looking out and looking backward...
I would not even
recognize...me!!!

A mask of God
is who I be...be...be!

You Can Do It

A small acorn once looked above it to see a great oak tree...
And said, "Oh, if only I could one day look like that!"
His friend the squirrel said...
"You know I have seen much...and I've seen a lotta ground!
Let me tell you... You can do it!"

Further in the forest, a drop of water from a pristine brook,
spied a grand lake body of water... and said to his friend
the turtle, "Oh, if only I could one day look like that!"
His friend the turtle said...
You know I have seen much...and I've seen a lotta water!
Let me tell you... You can do it!"

Traveling deeper in the forest, a jagged pebble lying on hard
ground looked up and saw a great mountain...and said
"Oh if only I could one day look like that!"
His friend the goat said...
"You know I have seen much...and I've seen a lotta mountains!
Let me tell you... You can do it!"

So friends, whether you're on the Ground...up a Creek...
or at Rock Bottom...your guardian Angel is always near you
Saying...
"You know I have seen much...and I've seen a lotta dreams!
Let me tell you... You can do it!"

Fleeting Thoughts

As I ponder on this summer's eve...
the willow wisps of feeling's long past,
darting and running along memories buried deep
teasingly echoing..."Here Master!...Here Master!
Hold me in your thoughts for now...
I am what you wish to slumber in,
gain comfort, and surrender your mind
that I might spark tears long forgotten
or passions never tasted...
Linger in me...for I am the ride of your life.
Greater heights none has seen
nor harkened not to pits of abyss,
that I shall give you taste!
Brush me not away for I am the Dawn
of your many mirrored self!
Who knows greater your glories
than that which has animated your divine spark
of the many you's and them's that has always been
and forever remains the glorious and external you!
For are we not all that we perceived
ourselves not to be...for how can
you locate a midnight star...without
the aid of the perceived emptiness
that unfolds it?
If you have known not the darkness...
how can you walk towards the dawn?
If I have tasted the fruit of the vineyard...
have I also not tasted the vine that birthed it?
Then, how my beloved, shall you taste
the sweetness of love without the
tartness of it's surrounding light?

Many wonders you shall see...amid the beauty yet to be!
Selah

Devin

Little girl named Devin,
who without her smile
the sun wouldn't shine
the rivers wouldn't flow
and bread wouldn't leaven

It's only been recently
that God threw open
the doors of her Kingdom...
that men of earth...call "Heaven!"

You Ever Been Alone?

You ever been alone,
where your breath is your only companion
and your thoughts are your only anchor?

Have you ever been alone,
where the weight of your body is too
heavy to lift from your seat?
Where your eyelids seem too heavy too move?

Have you ever been alone,
where you had not even the will to cry...
where the thought of your family was
only to say goodbye?

Have you ever been alone,
where the bottom line of all these questions...
is that you asked your God
to bring you "Home?"
Selah

Joseph Returns'
(Africa's Prodigal Son)

Africa, India, the America's...
it matters not which
just another dark child's body
thrown in the burial ditch!

The eyes are dim
the pulse is shed
the life of the soul
has gone ahead

The father's of which
have been killed by their shores
there is none to bar
the beasts from the door!

Mother's have been robbed
of their minds
and their daughters now
act in kind

The sons were jailed
for deeds not done
and now languish in
prisons under this earthly sun

The gate left unguarded
our old fell quick
and all the wisdom they held
was wasted
as they could not pass the stick

The darker the pigment
the swifter the result
attracting the hatred
of this hidden serpent cult

The black man's rise
they fear more than hell
of the retribution they'll suffer
if their gods fail to dispel
the angel hiding unconscious...under that dark skinned veil!

Not to let him awaken
is the driven prize
regardless of the nations, cities, or countries
that have to meet their demise!

He is not to awaken
understand this true and clear
for he knows not his ancestry
that descends from the heavenly spheres

He is not to cry aloud
for help from his God within
for truly the Beast must
relinquish his thrones of sin

From galaxy's far
and from galaxy's near
his protectors now journey
with vengeance in their ear

To disable the beast
from devouring our brother's soul
by awakening him to his kinship
to Arch Angels of Old
Michael stands ready

with sword in his hand
and his Band of Mercy
that no dark soul can withstand

Gabriel positions his horn
to the ready
to guarantee Creation's message
comes through all unlove
rich and steady

Standing ready to guard
his back and front
Rafael and Uriel prepare their
soul saving ceremonial acts
that become as whirlwinds
scattering unloves soulless pacts

There is none but the Light
that will truly survive
for the darkness even
themselves... they will come to despise

A transmutation will take place
of darkness to light
as unlove moves to love in spite
of attempting to hide
the power of the blackman's embryonic
Creator's light

For how can unlove
not fall victim to
the Angelic shower of the
Creator's power?

Your true description
has been held from you

since ages untold
For having the knowledge of yourself
would force the beast to empty
his vaults of gold
and without that...
his slavery over you and yours...
his bloodline cannot hold!

His sorcery and magic
will begin to loose its grip
if the financial bonds on
you begin to slip

His hold on your belly
would also slip right through
when your health returns
to empower the "God" in you!

Your name's has been a secret
and was so for years
for multitudes have died, and will die
to keep your ancestors from you!

For you fly to low
for the eagle that you are
for none of your fathers
hail from this earthly star

Afar, afar
as they finally begin to near
Yes, your Angels are coming...
and my brother, they bear more
than your clumsy earthly spears!

The one that comes
shall unveil all (such) his might

that no rock will bear witness
to their headlong fright

The ground will hide
none from their just due
it will bear up the sin's
of their father's...
trying to tear your souls from you!

To cast over this earth
a soul freeing dew...
that will give all Loves
children a golden Christ hue

Father, Father I say this
to the fallen man
"Arise...Arise...and allow
the Christ presence in you
your Higher Self
to help you stand!"

And so it is!
Oh great Angels of Light
awaken to your destiny...
awaken to my voice
which sounds so familiar...
It is the voice of "Remembering!"

Holy Angel of Light
that resides within me
show thineseff in all
your splendid color...
Show me who I am...ending for a time
The questions that even I hold!

Selah

The Greatest Son

Yusef Ali, the greatest son
that shall ever be
warms his father's heart
from the continents to the sea

A delightful child
always smiling at the day
and watching in amazement
at his dog Speedy's
attempt to keep the big dogs at bay

Never been a better "T" ball player
that I have seen
who after the game
always got his dad
to go to McDonalds and give up the green

Been a lot of times
that I miss so much
seeing his little head go by
and just reachin out to touch

With the Saturday mornings
came Sara and Arial
parading through the house
looking for good stuff to unveil

And next we have TJ, Veda, and Crystal
on many a weekend nite
running, jumping , and hiding
all within Mother Brenda's sight

And let's not forget Rhett
a old school chum
who had no fear of height
and would climb the highest pole just for fun!

Yes those days have long past
and he's still a champion to me
for he always will be the greatest Son
that ever will be...to me!

Desire

Within the memory of the day's last past
that which is within masquerading
as noble virtue
stands disrobed as itself...
a simple longing for your smiles
refreshing dew
How say thou to a heart erupting
with anticipation of thine focused smile...
What sayest thou heart in response
Are thine palpitations a meaningful
clue as to my shyness?
Shall I suck deeply mine breath
to gather my repose?
or shall I not heed mine blood
vessels, and witness mine life force
exude itself and dissipate
in the earth beneath my feet...
or shall I command the atoms
of my body to forge a bridge
to thine heart space to deliver
it's cargo of passions sweetly
kindled...
How sayeth my beloved...deemed me
worthy to offer/present my cloak
to shelter the shadow of thine
smile from the Angel of smiles
once smiled...and delivered to the
abyss of forgotten longings...
May I offer my scarf to tabernacle
your crown from the harsh tears
of the earth that might dampen
the twinkle cascading from thine eye...

tell me whom harkens men of strong
brawn to carry away thine good
hopes...nay nay my beloved
although the earth fills deep
with assassins of the heart...
I position myself between and
betwixt thee and any ill fortune...
I stand ready to be the "glisten"
on the next raindrop thy witness...
I stand ready to be the sweetness
on the nectarine thy hold before
thy mouth to taste...
I stand ready to be the 1st faintness
of joy thy feeleth upon your morning's
first glance...
I stand ready to humble myself
for thine desires to mount and
beckon for passage to the
physical world of the scene...
as I stand ready to cast my lance
through the ghosts of your delusions...
I am at thy feet
in the sanctity of humble worship...
casting my self prostrate
to shield thine feet from the
dust that arrives with the hordes
of angels I have brought forth
to protect and shield the masses
of unbetrothed, from the dazzling
radiance emanating from the comers
of thine eyes as you witness the
"first coming" of my tears of joy
for you!

How Small Is A Thought

Man's inability to think
is his demise
Man's unwillingness to forgive
is his disaster
Man's refusal to protect
is his destruction
Man's surrendering to pride
is his damnation

His demise was brought upon
by unthinking
His disasters come to him from
his unwillingness to forgive
His destruction overtakes him by
refusing to protect his progeny
And most importantly, his damnation
follows his coattails of pride
into the abyss of his ego!

Shadow

Don't be afraid of the Shadow
for it is truly you

Don't be afraid of the Shadow
for its realm is the darkness too...

Don't be afraid of the Shadow
for it moves only when you do

And above all don't be afraid of the Shadow...
for it is your teacher of
those lessons...you choose not
to look to God to!

Let it be acknowledged that...
if you keep God in front of you
the shadow will always stay behind thee...

If you put yourself ahead of God
the shadow will always lead the way...

And if you allow God to only walk
side by side of you...then the shadow
will walk side by side of you too!

Remember the shadow will always take you
places you may not choose to go...
it is not God...it is like you...
it doesn't know
the way either!!!

Water's Near

When the ocean cries
a waterfall appears
just beyond the rainbow's
highest tier...

A fog rolls in
on the first dawn's light
unveiling playful dolphins awakening
from their night

The citizens of the deep
appear never to sleep
while they guard their treasures
never meant for mankind to reap

A great mass of wetness
a psychic may peer
as a child wets her hair
playing in hidden coves near...

In other places great ships
make their way
to islands where breezes and men
meet to play

Somewhere I know there is a lesson
in here...
If I can but gather the courage
my soul would cheer...

As I face
my childhood fear of abandonment
that always evokes my
deepest tears!

In A Stranger's Ear

In a stranger's ear
we can share our innermost fear
describe a delicious moment
that bring about ecstatic tears

We can cover
ourselves with glory abound
and perch our bodies
in higher places where
eagles cannot be found

In a stranger's ear
our identity can be who we choose
as long as we stroke
the entity listening with proper ado

No, none has ever been
a criminal in a stranger's ear
Because there again
your ego relishes its power
with the one straining to hear

And truly it is a shame
this coming from one who knows,
that the one truly listening
has the power to shut
all the heavenly doors (dozes)

In other words
How can you tell a stranger the truth
and your Father a lie
He's really not that far away you know,
up in that imaginary sky...
Because a inch above your
eyebrow...
is really not that very high!!!

Voyager 1

The river moves behind thee...
yea, but a shadow of waters long past
The mountains stand before thee
and waiver not in the shadows they cast

And in your presence...
right now where you stand
what manner of God...
what manner of man?

Apology's

I apologize once
maybe I'll do it twice
for my actions of the past
weren't very nice

So I'll say it again too
this time in full view
the sweetness of your heart
Didn't receive it's full due

Ponder closely my beloved...
do you see
the God in
You?

Along For The Ride

Will you ride the bicycle
of life with me?
I'll push the pedals
if you steer and see...
And if a time comes
between the mountains of life...
and the blissful sea
We'll switch roles
and it will be my turn
to look out for thee!

And as we reach
our graying years of sunset
we'll "trade in" the old bicycle of life...
for a brand new spiritual
red "corvette!"

A Woman's Heart

I desire thy breast
not to suckle and harness...
but to caress the compassion
that lies within

Thy heart directs royal bloodlines
to flow to destinations
that requireth the sustenance
of its vessels

Mine thoughts are with thee
from eyebrow to heel
I awaiteth only thy nod
to loose mine limbs
to cherish and lift thee up
to the thrones of the heavens.

I know not a plan
nor have I measured the way...
I respectfully submit to God's guidance
to come what may!

So as I reach for thy breast...
draw not away
for it is only your heart
that I (desireth) hunger this day!

Keep Steppin

Hi days and low days
follow one by one
till some life sunsets
appear to darken all the fun
Keep steppin!

Health is good today
you feel mighty fine
till a doctor friend
tells you your life's
on the line
Keep steppin!

Been married once or twice
maybe this is the 1st time
Then you come home
to read a note
that the relationship is done...
Keep steppin!

Or done piled a bunch of money
and its stacked in the bank real high...
then you get a call from your broker
that your nest egg has gone Bye-bye...
Keep steppin!

Here's a thought,
you know the case in court
you won the other day...
Well, the prosecutor appealed
and the arresting officers
are on the way...
Keep steppin!

How about yesterday
when you helped the elderly man...
Seems he lost his keys
and was locked out of his van...
Well, when he grabbed in appreciation
your hand
seems he had caught a deadly virus...
and died in a ten minute span...
Now they are cutting out your tombstone...
Have you noticed your swollen glands?
Keep steppin!

Maybe nothing so drastic
as bankruptcy, divorce, or suicide
maybe just maybe
your preacher just told you in 2 days
the earth and the sun will collide...
if Oral Roberts don't get in there
and turn the tide!
My beloved, just remember to put
your head back
and take it in stride...
and maybe we'll hit a meteor
or maybe it might go wide!
Keep steppin!!!

When you look back over your journey
at the end of the line...
You can clearly see
my beloved
you were being carried
all the time!
Keep steppin!!!

Introduction to Gabriel's Bell

Gather my beloved...
gather near...
for I have a grand truth tale
right now for your ears...

Tis about lust...and vice...
and greed farand near!
When the man with the rum
enslaved the man with the spear...

Tis about arrogance and passions
bringing them to the brink
of sinful disasters
where they now sink
as the human heart confronts the lie...
that it is not extinct!

So gather my beloved...
hold back your fears
for the time will come to humble me
with your tears...

This day however,
I rejoice in your touch
of sharing a message
that for me means so much...

Tis a day of rejoicing...
some Say it might be
but I'll choose my words carefully
for I want you to see...

How my ancestors...your ancestors
clandestinely lit
a fire so bold it defies extinguishing
even by God's own spit

Hate and guilt
now burn so high
that generations are born
heaving a deep sigh!
Masters and slave's blood
has long been combined...
that now it resembles
a Rothchild's fine wine

Blended here
and from young vines torn
that none in human form
can with a race themselves adorn!

Divinely meshed
and divinely blessed...
Mankind now represents
the jewels of a celestial pirate's chest

But alas, my beloved
man is a troubled sort...
For Angels of darkness
with him now make sport!

His lust and fears
grant them rich soil...
Now his heart they would like
for his love to spoil...

Harken human
and drop your mask...
for unlove is poised
ready and willing
to put your earthly generation to task!

Hear well these sounding's...
"That which is ...has been
That which was...will be
That which will be...is present this day..."

Now gather near...
and hear me well
about a dark day past,
as I shall recount the story
of Gabriel's Bell.

Ding...Ding...Ding!

A Tear

Have you ever walked away from a tear... -
That was caused
while thinking of a loved one
so dear?

Putting all your other emotions
in a higher gear?

And when you wiped it away
you could still feel the fear?

As it fell to the ground
shaking your world to your rear?

Making you just want to scream to the heavens
"Please tell God, I'm not here!"

Lawd
(Daddy's preah)

Done did all I knows
don't knows no mo
pain get fearsome
wont let me go!

The chilluns is fine
running all over my feets
missus wants 'nother
but we's runnin out-a-sheets!

Ole dog jus sits
got ole you know
I shows him the birds
all he do, is jus rollover and sno(re)!

Lawd, I jus wanted to tell you
caus I knows you get busy... (I) know
I jes hav'in to do this sometimes,
so I can minds myself, that you's runnin the show!

So, I'm gonna put this here hat back on...
and walk back down this hill...
Jes, if you don't mind... me freshin yo mind
to (re) member we's in Jesus's will!

Selah

Sayin What's Right!

I's been tole
massa Callin us hissin black gole...
I guess ole massa
he oughta know...
Him an his peoples been stealing us
from before I know!

He got da blood from the turnip
as his big house shows
Always talkin wild bout how
his black gole fill'im full of woes!

Says he owns the land far
as he can see...
Wonder ifn his soul hurt like mines
when I looks at my little Dee?

Can't run to far
ain't no where to go...
Here tell his peoples
runs the whole strange land from sho(re) to sho(re)

I guess I don't minds really
be'un massa's black gole...
Caus unless massa don't change his ways
it's gonna cost him his soul!

Yo knows a man might have money...
and land he calls his yo knows
But ifn he ain't got God in his heart and "actin"
then he done lost the only thang that really
matters...
The man done lost his soul!

Selah

Your Smile

Seeing your smile...
is like witnessing
a glorious
summer morning's dawn!

Only the brilliance of your eyes
casts paleness
on the inspiration of light dancing
over Earths silhouetted edge.

What matters the night...
now, but a after thought
given life by an illusionary facade
cloaked in the cloth of past intent...

What matterest a beam of light
already well beyond
the witnesses anticipated glance?

Who...
among you
describeth a vision faded
to it's author's memory?

Or who passeth
a sweet tongues taste
to his neighbors mouth
satisfactorily?

So be it...
descriptions of your smile
longingly linger past millenniums of languages

both forgotten and past...
Be ye goddess...
I know not!
But by the sanctions of Heaven
knoweth thou possesseth
the smile of my Creation's God!

Selah

Standing Alone

Like a broken figurine
I stand alone...lonely
while witnessing
my beloved take possession of another!

My constant longing for thine
stretches as a worm pit
deep towards the bowels
of this earth

Were it not for the physics
of this mound...
my sorrow would traverse
the parameters of this earthly shore
to the sands of another land
on a distant world...

Who sanctions the measure of desire
when tipped beyond the human minds edge?
What say thee beloved...
why does thou seeketh me not?

Knoweth not I harbour
the seeds of thy soul's escaping bliss?
Thou knowest not...thy protector
shadowing thy fragile womb?

Thou knowest not...thy twin of
Angelic/heavenly spirit and desire?
Has the mask of thy bruised ego
hiddeth my countenance behind
it's shadow?

Knowest-not love
as its poured
from mine eye
to thine lap...and feet?

Does thou desireth my tears to race
to caress and dampen warmly
that part of thee...that gives thee flight
to another's affection?

Thy desireth more...
what sayeth thou?
Speaketh
and it shall be done...

Gesture...
and my servants
the Princes of the earth
will relieve thy burdens...

Ponder...
and my brothers in Heaven
will unveil wonders
your heart never perceived... -
What sayeth thou?

Deem it so..
and I will reroute thy blood vessels
to carry good health to your heart..
to still the excitement
that lies deep within thy womb

Deem it so...
and I will cause a bridge to be formed
between us
that will deliver my life essence
to thy weary parts
What say thou beloved?

Or do thee desireth thy servant
to restoreth thine hearing
that has long since turneth it's deafness
from me to God...

And lastly...
"My Most Elusive Desire"
with the help of the heavens..
thine servant will restore the light
to thy soul...and plant thee back again
in God's bosom...
What sayeth thou?

Thinking of Thee

As I think of thee...
my bodies essence
seepeth from it's confines
Reach for me...
and capture my bounty,
before its defiled by the silks
that encapsulate my hips!
For its source
is minute in volume...
However, its fruit holds testimony
of Heaven and Earth's ordained Cosmos...
Even life unrecognized seeks its favor!

Selah

A Lost Love Remembered

Remembering a lost love
is like witnessing a candle newly lit
and later viewing the candles empty wick...
who knowest the destination of the wax...
who knowest thy heart once lit...where it stirs
and where and with whom
it finally retires?

Selah

How Big Is Your Dream

Dreams are like water...
they have not form
until placed into a container...
then it mimics
the limits and parameters
of which it is bound

In what space
do you hold your dreams...
have you given it room to hold
more of itself
or
must the limitations of your container
cause its fruit to seek another?

Just as the water of this earth
is more cherished than fine gold
do you present a teacup to be filled...
or
do you present the Heaven above
to be your receptacle?

A sip
will answer my thirst,
however, a pool is needed
for my cleansing

Am I not
a child of the Heavens...
then...how shall you limit
ME?

Selah

Awaken

Awaken sweet Angels
the time is here
Humans need you near
to comfort them in their fears

Only our Creator
knows their plight...
but you have been sent
to even the fight

Radiating love
that for sure will tumble...
those that are here
to cause man to stumble!

Open your eyes
that man may see...
his celestial help
that for him holds the key
to reclaiming his soul
from the unlove
that he cannot see!

If only for a moment
as you lift thine wing
your sight will give man cause
for a new song to sing

It's not that he's weak...
for man is a mighty race
the truth be known...
he knows not who to chase

But now that you're awake
his fortune will change
his captors now know
their work was in vain

For when the Angels show up
their omnipotence fades...
because their true selves are seen
in the full darkness of the shade

Now that you...the Creator's Angels
are in the plan
how can they stand...
when you...the Forces of Light
become Mankind's righteous hands?

Selah

The Greatest Poem I Ever Wrote

The greatest poem I ever wrote
was not penned in ink...
The greatest poem I ever wrote
was scribed with the intent of the heart to link
my passions and the heavens
before God called forth my eyelids last blink!

So many times past
I felt I lost my way
until spirit enlivened my consciousness
giving me a broader horizon for my Soul to play

Sometimes a word may not due
As I lay my thoughts to rest
I can only hamess a feeling
before my Sun turns its direction west

As the morning's dawn hints from the east
my longings begin to stir
as I make peace with my shadow's beast
Remembering well...that all within man must concur

Whether it's the animals of the earth
or the fowl of the air
we all forget sometimes that
this land is here for all to share

The greatest poem I ever wrote
began in despair
with my tears flooding my pillow without care
as self abuse laid open my Soul to bare

The greatest poem I ever wrote
was and continues to be
the saga of my spirit
being set free
by the God of Light
that evermore resides in me!
Selah

A Warrior's Prayer

Oh great warrior
who calleth the God in me
to unveil itself
To render my bodiments untouchable
by human form
and cause the piercing of my eye
to evacuate all foe before me
that I survey

Oh greatest of warriors
whom justice cherishes greatly...
Still my bow
that I may know repose

For the children of the vanquished
slumber not in their revenges...
And only by thine offering
"loves soothing salves"
that arrows adorn not my back

Oh greatest of all warriors
flower your peace among my rivals...
that we may banquet at the table
of the justice wine
and savor the meats of abundance
in brotherhood...
as we wed our women of piety

Touch not the gray that jewels my head...
for in proper stead
eventually even the worms of this shell
must also be fed

Oh yes, oh great one...
that will be a joyful time
as my body reforms itself into the earth
as Heaven's noon day reaches it's highest chime

Spirit

I am Spirit
I cannot be contained
I can be trapped for a time
but you hold me at your own peril!

I do not fade
I do not die
I am eternal
I always expand

I am Spirit
I am all that you perceive
I am all that you believe
I live!

I am all that you be
However, I am more than you see...
I animate your smallest cell
I am your highest concept of God

I am Spirit
I am simply what I am
I am Love
I am... I am...

I am whatever follows "I am" in your descriptions
I always make it simple
I begin your sentence...
and I allow you to finish it!

Knowing

How can one know sweetness
if he has never held a child?

How can passion be felt
if your lusts have never stirred?

How can one know love
if she has never been unconditionally held

How can one know sorrow
if she has never tasted her tears?

How can...How can...How can...

Simply by being...Simply by being...Simply by being!
Selah

Can You Help Me?

Can't describe what I'm feelin
Can you help me?
Please be judgmental...
Please be condescending...
Please be cutting...
Yes, please be the real you this righteous day...

Please be shallow
Please be conceited
Please be condemning
Yes, please be the real you this righteous day...

Look deeply...
What do you see?
Oh, by the way
Do you like the mirror I hold before me
this righteous day?
Selah

Dinner Party

Last night I had dinner...
Jesus brought the wine
The Brotherhood of Heaven
brought the meatless meat
John brought the honey
and Mary brought the sweets!

Pharaoh brought the servants
Abraham brought his sons
Joseph prepared the menu
and Solomon thought
He was the one
Goliath watched my back
while David watched the front
Judas gave directions and the
straightest path to my door
As Paul walked my shorelines
helping my ships ashore

Moses brought golden instructions
on how long my dinner should last
and my host washed my feet
of guilt/remorse I held on from the past!

And yes...while the wine was good
and the meatless meat tasted as delicious
as the honey and sweets

And yes...the servants, sons, and
menu all came together in song

While Goliath watched by back
and David watched my chest
Judas gave directions...
and Paul gave me his best

And alas Moses talked all night
about some kinda golden calf...
as God just held my feet
and gestured and laughed,
Saying don't worry my Son...
You're right...this dream won't last!

This Ain't No Rhyme

"Hi Diddle Diddle"...
I ain't never seen a "Cat play a Fiddle"
and I ain't never seen a "Cow jump over the Moon!"

But I have seen a Dove paint a rainbow
and a Frog lead a symphony

Now I can't imagine
"Jack climbing no Beanstalk"
or a "Wolf
blowing down a Pig's house!"

But I'll bet
all the money in my pocket
that a smile will ease your pain
and a Dolphin's kiss will change your life!

And no, I don't want a "Rose Garden"...
or a "Lily from the Field"
I'd really prefer to set in awe
and watch God create
when I just sit still...

I heard "Little Orphan Annie"
got married just the other day...
seems she met the son of "Dagwood"
at a local Chinese buffet

But there's one thing I do believe
and this is coming from the heart...
that believing in our own resurrection
is the "one and only place"

Mankind can start
...Without proverbially
"Putting the horse before the Cart!"
Selah

Once Upon A Time

Once upon a time...
I died...and was awakened
Once upon a time
I was awakened...and then I died!

Who says death is not the illusion
of a unawakened man
Who says an unawakened man
is not the illusion of the dead?

Once upon a time...
a woman lived
a woman died
a woman was awakened!

Once upon a time...
the Awakened Ones
lifted a woman in death...
and she lives!

Once upon a time...
the Awakened Ones lifted up the Unawakened Ones...
and they Live!!!

Selah

A Lesson

A wise man once taught me
that Mankind's inner faith
is like a perfectly rounded ball
which moves along smoothly
until it runs into a wall...
which it implants itself
until another of kind disposition
points it in another direction
with a push of momentum (compassion)

What wall do you face?
and have you asked for (the way) direction?
Then...
why don't you move?

Here's a lesson,
Inner Faith does not...
will not...
serve you until
"You" point "It" in the right direction!
Selah

Being Born

While born of Man...
I humanly be!
While born of God
I celestially see

While born of flesh...
I seek joy for thee
While born of Spirit...
I know peace is the Key!
Selah

Paradox's

You witness...
but you don't see
You touch...
but you don't feel
You laugh...
but you don't have joy
You hope...
but you don't have any faith

You cry...
but you don't feel sadness
and you won't let me comfort you

You suffer...
but you don't know pain
and you won't ask for help

You wish...
but you don't dare to hope

You judge...
but real perception escapes you

You covet
but you don't recognize jealously

You die...
but you don't know how to "let go!"

You fly...
but you refuse to let yourself soar

And above all my beloved

You "are" lost...
but you wont let me guide you

You ask to "Know" me...
but you are afraid to look!

What say ye?
Selah

How Deep Is The Sand

How deep...How deep...
How deep can you hide your head?
How deep...How deep...
How deep until you can hide your feet?

Say don't want to be seen
Dig a little deeper
Say you don't want to be heard
Dig a little deeper!

How deep...How deep
How deep can you go?
How deep...How deep
How deep must you go...
before you forget what you know?

Tie a string around your finger...
so you wont forget
who is trying to tie a rope
around your neck!

Playah...Playah...
Stand up tall
Because who you're hiding from
means to kill your children
one and all!

They all can't hide...
nor can they all stand "still"
while the dark ones salivate
as they enforce their "will!"

You need to go deeper...
make it long and wide
cause we got 26 million
from the beast we need to hide!

So how deep...how deep...
Shall you go in your pit
till you finally figure it out
"That We All Can't Fit?"

Old Wineskins/New Wine

What means a valentine
when you are ancient of days...
and your flower of desire
is but near her first spring of Life?

Who harkens to desires
contained in a wineskin
long creased
with age?

Doth not new flowers
crave rich vibrant soil
newly tilled
as of late?

Be it possible
for it to reach and impregnate
a bud near its
last season's peak?

Is it possible for the great oak
shadowing the flower not far from its first spring...
to parent the needs
of that flowers 1st bloom?

Nay, Nay...the great Oak
just as the oceans of ancient water
continually transitioning to destinations before
them...
is but a vessel of repose (protection) and retreat for
the new flowers...
new in stem...nursed and protected in it's shadow!

For whom may challenge
the wisdom of the great Oak...
that possesseth root within the earth
running long and deep?

What foolishness
can present itself
that has been unseen
by Him?

Even the mushrooms
of seasonal delicate taste
hovers near the great Oak's
nurturing bosom...

Seemingly possible the beautiful rose
under its canopy will whither from inattention...
or needeth it another rose likened to itself
to commune the vibrancy and excitement of its earthly
experience...

Be it the sum of all Love...
to nurture...
empower...
and protect

Be it the role of all old wineskins
to harbor their delicate treasures
in the excitement of their youth...
to the maturity of their last drops tasted!

So be it!

Deceit

Once deceit enters a bond
the heart begins to calcify
towards its author...
until its hardened against all
warm memory

Love combined with forgiveness
becomes the only
softening agent
prescribed for the Broken of Heart

Like unto Trust
once given
the recipients only issue
is Yea or Nay...

As with any gift
the value lies
with the intent of its author...
Thou can present only
the content of ones heart...
All else is folly!

Immortal You

You have never been born...
you have never died...
You always have been
And you always shall be!

Names die
forms cease to be
And all illusions dissipate
The "you" that animates all the above is eternally present!

A Time of Pain

I have look at fear...
it is an awesome bluff
Causing some to give up their ghost
Thinking they're not enough

I have looked at fear
sometimes causing me to quiver
when contemplating relief
even now my fingers begin to shiver

A coward I am not
no that's not the case
I just lingered to long
with fear in my face

I reach for strength
that sometimes I'm sure
is not there...
But then my body releases
from somewhere within
a courage it can share

As I sit here writing
knowing not the next word
God steadies my hand
for the next noun or verb...

It must be funny
being one of great wit...
to witness my shaking hand
dancing from a word
to a paragraph timely writ

Some say its an art
I don't know if this is true
But my arm steadies a bit
when given revelations that
in time become due!

Help me...Help me...
I say in my soul
Help me...Help me
I find my spirit standing in gold

I tire of the drama
which always leads to more
I tire of the trauma
that lies in sight of my door

A hapless victim...
no I say this not
Rather a fear driven soul
which returneth always
to the same spot

I relinquish the pain
that I now find in my soul
I reach out to touch
the Godly presence that transcends
times of new and old!

I cease the bantering
for it avails me not...
I seek solace in the knowing
that God's love extends far beyond
my pens last jot!

By now...I assume
you can feel my awesome pain
as it covers all about me
as a harsh winter's rain

But there is comfort
and this is coming from within
an eternal peace is birthing
the Christ whose words at first begin

I am the Way...the Truth...and the Light
Stand still...and feel the Truth
Stand still...and feel the Way
Stand still...and feel the Light
Peace...Peace...Peace....
Feel it and Be Still
for it is our Creator's Will!"

A Child's Hope

One day last week
on Wednesday morn
a child lost hope
after a siblings scorn

The earth shifted
and the rocks settled low
while in desperation
to aid the child in a safe path to go

The winds rustled the leaves
while the pebbles made a row
to give a dove an easy tread
so peace the child could know

The water's parted slightly
and the rainbows pointed the way
As this child's heart was redeemed
on this beautiful Easter's day
bringing tears to even the Angels
as the child was heard to say
Telling his father..."Fear not!"
"The Christ is here this day
and in His love and protection
there is no human sway!"

The Christ has taken my hand
and in His strength I have leaned
So again I dare to hope...
And so again... I dare to dream!

What I Want

I want to save the world
but words are my only raft
I want to feed the hungry
but truth is my only craft

I want to house the homeless
but my words
can only shelter you
in hope

I want to cure the addicted
but I don't know
if my poetry can help
you cope

I want to help the dying
but my pen
only buries
the lies

I want to expose corruption
but my paragraphs
only bring up
more ties

I want to replace anger with joy
but my Light illumines
the darkness
and those they wish to destroy

I want to do so much
but my fingers
grow weary...
as you might guess

For what human
without the Christ
can pass through
the "Jesus" test?

A Gentle Thought

This day I met my wife
for me she took the "L" out of "Lonely"
so with confidence...
I removed the "e" from "Me"...
Now she's my "one and only!

Tryin To Figure It Out

Know it all...
I don't know nothing
Seen it all...
I ain't seen nothing
Heard it all...
I ain't heard nothing
Done it all...
I ain't done nothing

Well I know
what I have seen...
I know what I've heard...
and I know what I've done!

But for the life of me...
God has yet to divulge
what it all means
and let "me" in on the fun!!!

Selah

Asking A Question

I am standing on this precipice...
facing "my" world asking
"What wants to happen?...What do you choose to happen?

My world answered with a booming baritone
and a sweetly shrilling ring following each note
Saying " I Simply Choose To Be!"...
See me...feel me...touch me...
I simply choose to be...
Don't look away...
Look at me with courage...
My mountains...Rivers...and Sky!
We simply choose to be...

Now look again quickly...
"Facing me with courage...What do you wish to See?"

Challenges

I'm scared of rocks
But I like to climb mountains
I don't like water
But I swim in the oceans

I don't trust the air
But often I jump off cliffs
I don't like to sleep
But I always dream as I walk

I'm a paradox
But I guess
that is what being human
is all about!

Show me right
and I turn left
Gesture upwards
and I lay down

Tell me I can't do it...
And I'm the 1st in line
How else in Heaven...
Can I let this light inside me shine?

The Request

We can ask for help so much
that God will stop sending us ships...
And will simply remove us
from our self created world...

The simple minded call it "Dying!" -

Reality

I saw a bird
I guess he got tired of flying
and died in the sky
when he fell to earth...
he simply rolled over
got up
and walked away!

We can't assume our neighbors reality is ours on any
given day...
Who says blue jays can't play soccer?
Who says your reality is his anyway?

The Strongman and The Baby

I once saw a great strong man
hold a tiny baby...he was very tender!
Sometimes our greatest strengths lie just
behind our greatest illusion...Be Tender!

Be like the strongman...
When weakness shows up "in" you
hug...cuddle...and show the greatest tenderness
to "yourself!"

We all give the illusion
of the "strongman"...
However, we all seek unconditional love
like the "baby!"

Where is the greatest lesson?
In the one "holding"...
or the one being "held?"
In the "forgiver"..
or the one being "forgiven?"

In the Strongman...or the baby?

What masks do we wear today...
My Angels?

Selah

A Lonely Time

As I stand among humanity's masses
surveying the horizon for hope...
My eyes grow weary and
my thoughts grow blurry...
Harder yet, it becomes
weighty to articulate
optimistic verse...

The blood which only moments
before careened from vessel to
vessel...and vein to vein
now humbles me with its pace
beckoning itself to a standstill...

Anxiety creeps forward as the
warrior within seeks slumber
as his strength of knee fails him
and hibernates in its domicile
of fear...

Eyelids once fluttering within
nanoseconds of time...
Now cause themselves to narrow only
when shadows bright pose themselves
as vague...

Whom knowest the arrival of symbols
of hope...
Bearing the fruits of their thoughts
brightly formed...

As a new dawn always bring the Sun
so too does hope birth anticipated joys...

and as sages ancient of days
and birthed on yester morn
All verily offer testimony that
thy help arriveth without fail
at the dawn of your gentle hearts
first moment of awake...
How knoweth I?

Yea, that be answered only, by my soul
which peereth through dimensions of
time and actions...
As does a light beam through
whispers of fog!

Only my heart rendereth the song of
my soul to thy human ear...
No...Nay not I ...ever-now or before...
Decipher and explain the celestial
language of its timeless domain...

I can only listen as thou to perceive
its teachings...
Do I say I am mute...no nay that not
be the case...
Does thou say I be deaf...no nay I pray tell
neither is this truth...
Thus saith I...and this be my heavenly
intent...
One heart speaketh as to the many for
in this place of humanity's home...
We all be of one heart...one body...
and only one celestial mind

This...thus we have forgotten
This...thus is the message of the
one heart...
Looketh upon the dawn

for my messengers of joy are being led
by love which cloaketh all in its
stead with its oneness of purpose...
invoking all of us to slumber in its
peace of mind!

Where to go...there is no destination!
What to do...there is no act to be done!

The celestial soul giveth peace to all of
itself while residing in its realm of
being...that allows it to partake of
the Mother of all actions...Simply choosing
to "Be!"

The Father of all earthly actions
is non-action...just as the definition of
all earthly form is the area around it.
Bearing our definition of no form...or simply
put...Empty space must be present to define
a place of form...or filled space!
Thus saith Soul!

There is always a lonely time in
every mans/woman's heart directly
proceeding a profound new dawning
from a night of the Soul...
That time when all appears to be lost
and the spirit lifts its eyes to higher
perception...and heralds
my Angels ride to me swiftly
over the piercing light beams
of the 1st dawn's light...
Rescuing me from the separation
of the darkness...and
from this "Lonely Time!"

Selah

Differences

A rose of a different garden...
is still a rose!
A horse of a different herd...
is still a horse!
A coat of a different fabric...
is still a coat!
A dog of a different breed...
is still a dog!
A bird of a different feather...
is still a bird!
A word of a different language...
is still a word!
A book of a different cover...
is still a book!
And how say it...
A brother of a different soil
be "not" your brother?

I once saw a poet
coming towards me with a huge pen...
We nodded...
He walked past me
I never saw him again!

We ask
for "real" love so hard
that when it shows up...
we never recognize it!

Remember...your life is like
a drinking well!
You have to guard what goes into it.
Because eventually...you will have to
drink from it!

Daily life is like a road...
All roads will get you somewhere
The smoother they are
you are more apt
to fall asleep at the wheel...
However...a bumpy road will always
keep your eyes wide open!
Question is...
"Do you really want to sleep through it?"

Trying to avoid
the "Dramas and Traumas" of life...
Is like driving on a mountain road
and not reading the signs...

Even if you make it safely
to the top...
You have to travel
the same road again...
to get back
"down!"

Doing a kind deed for a child...
Is like giving a farmer a delicious
red apple...
Not only can "he" enjoy its sweetness
but from its seeds...
His family and his family's family
can savor the deliciousness of its fruit
on "yonder's morrow!"

The pressure of daily living
left unmanaged
can push the body into oblivion...

Or with balance and prayer
can cause you to be a great jewel
for your family

Such as the pressure of the physical earth produces
first "coal"...which has its uses...
then intensifies to transform that coal
into a 'brilliant diamond!"

When you feel your weakest
and with least control...
Is when
your Guardian Angel takes over,
And that's really when
"God"
has his best opportunity
to work!

The difference
between a Blind man walking
down a road
and a Good sighted man...

Is the Blind man knows
he must listen
"for guidance"...
While the Good Sighted man
listens
"only to himself!"

Women meditate
Men seek the sensible
while Children just tell the truth!

Evil is the dark reflection of life
and as one lives...
He reflects both
his "Light" and his "Shadow"
during his span of years!

Dreaming is like experiencing sex...
You don't figure it out
until its over
when you finally
sit up!

A devoted mate is like a
hand with one wedding ring...
It don't quite fit until you've
worn it for a while!
while the other highlights the heart!

A pretty woman is like a
diamond ring...
"One" highlights the hand.

Simple truth
comes in many disguises...
Simplicity
is not one of them!

If two feet on the ground makes
a man more stable...
Then what is he with one foot on
the ground...and one
foot in his mouth?

Good intent, knowledge, and spiritual
intuition is a good recipe for sadness...
It's always sadness when God pulls
you to leave your pack!

I say today...
that there can only be
4 dominant frogs in your lake,
each with their own direction...
And they causeth all to follow them in
one way or another!

A whip
and a fool's tongue
are one and the same...
They both
always leave scars!

Playing with animals
is like dipping one's hand
in a cool pool...
It satisfies the soul!

Talking with a pretty soul is like
having a mouthful of mashed
potatoes...
they both are easy
to swallow!

The hardest soul to convince
on any subject...
Is the one staring back at you
from the mirror!

The only thing similar about the experience
of the words
"Death" and "Defeat"...
Are they both begin
with the letter "D!"

When writing...
my Soul is the pen
and my Body is the ink!
What would you have me say?

The truth
about your "Shadow self'...
Is he is "lost" too!
Are they not
always following
"you?"

It is said...
"Your life drama's will ease
when your Shadow shakes your hand"...
I say..."Be Bold"
you turn around and shake "his!"

Lust and Alcohol are not the same...
When an Alcoholic dies
his craving ceases...
When a "man of lust" dies
his appetite still longs
to be quenched!

Human Beings
are like cars
unless you get close...
You cannot tell
"who"
is driving it!

A "Little" dog barks
to get attention...
A "Big" dog
don't have to bark!

The only difference between
a rabbit in the cooking pot
and the rabbit running free...
Is one didn't hesitate!

The greatest lesson in watching
a Sunset or a Sunrise...
Is witnessing that the Sun doesn't
stop until it gets where it's going!

Observing beauty is like one
looking into a mirror...
Its always the observer who
makes the judgment!

Regarding pain...
Physical pain can be devastating,
however, psychological pain
oftentimes is "crippling!"

Judging another is akin to
reaching for a bee's honey with the naked hand...
Not unlike the naked ego.
If you attempt to claim another's
"honey"...You will get stung!
Leave your judgment ...like honey collection...
to the professionals.
And you won't expose yourself to pain!
Water is the glue of all earthly life...
Love is the glue of Spirit!

A shaking tree is held by it's root...
A nervous spirit is grounded by it's soul!

The pain of disappointment...
can only be soothed by the ointment
of new hope!

If a cat has 9 lives...
then what is the legacy of a man?
Only the unawakened relegate
their earthly experience to
only "one?"

Forgiveness is like Tenderness...
Its most welcome when we
feel our "worst!"

Racism is like a seed...
It won't grow unless you nourish it!

Friendship is like a sunbeam...
it warms you all over on your "stormiest "days!

God sends his fisherman to the sea
where they can cast their nets...
bless their bounty and release
those not ready to be harvested!

It is further said that God doesn't
send his fisherman to the desert
because they can't cast their nets...
And the fish don't like the sand!

Don't be surprised
when walking
on your charted path
that you are being followed...

Because remember,
Just as a candle in a cave
gives the "lost" hope

Your brother is secretly
looking for the way out too...
You may be the only
"light"
he will ever see!

So why not follow discreetly
at a safe distance behind thee?
Because like all caves
it's always lonely in the dark!

And as they gather courage
to step on your path of light
those that they pass
excitedly follow...
because they
don't want to be "left behind"
either!

Children are like ships
sometimes caught on
strong currents...

The greatest support you may
be able to give,
is to help "them" correct
their course!

Who knoweth the
breeze upon thy
cheek...
But for memories
past of thy
blowing
winds!

How can thou give word
to a unexperienced
event...
What saith thou?

Unless you have removed
thy shielding from thy own breast...
How can thy ever know a
warm bosom?

We ask for "real" love so hard
that when it shows up...
we never recognize it!

Remember...your life is like
a drinking well!
You have to guard what goes into it.
Because eventually...you will have to
fill your own cup!

Man like the great oak tree...
reaches only his
full height when following
his true nature...
or Divine Design!

The Divine Design of each man
is his roadmap to
exquisite "joy!"

Embarking on your road to
your Divine Design
is kinda scary...
it's akin to your mother
cutting your birth cord
and telling you
"Well, I got you this far...
have a good life!

If you are not being what
you were born to be...
and doing what you
were made to do...
Then why did
you come?

There is "no thing" on this earth
that one man can accomplish
that another man cannot...
"Given all other factors & circumstances
being alike!

The only question man must answer
in his heart is...
Do I truly desire wisdom & light
or is it a passing fancy...

Answer this 1st...then proceed as thy will!!!

The jurisdiction of the heart
knows no bounds...
only ones mind puts forth the fences

An Angel is simply no more than
an "uplifted" you!

If you look at pain as your band-aid
then there's no confusion
as to why you're wrapped spiritually from
"head to toe"
as a Egyptian mummy!

You cannot dip the toe into the water
to test its temperature...
without the whole body shivering from it!

Hope is the soul's salve/ointment
for human despair!

You, like the pebble lying in the road,
didn't start out by itself...
it was like you
a part of a greater whole...
and then found itself cut off
and seemingly alone!

The only issue that human man has...
is believing that he too is God...
"like his Father!"

Milk is only sweet to him that has a taste
for milk...
For those who thirst for honey
milk is sour!

The greatest man among you
in their own beginnings...
could not hold their
own bowel!

If you have eyes to see...
ears to hear...
and a mouth to taste

One of your elder bretheren
wiped your tears...
whispered they loved you...
and soothed your fears...
then fed you from their breast
until you were reared

Now...why don't you feel blessed?

Discipline is only tempered by your desire!

An empty page is a poets best work!

That which I fear stalks me!

My true self lies between
the space of two heartbeats...
the heartbeats remind it only
of its human boundaries!

Being scared of being loved
is akin to cursing your
body for breathing!

I know of no man
as proper as he may be...
who may go a fort night
without toileting!

The man who can carry
his own wealth with him
is in far better condition...
than a rich man...
who must depend on others
to carry his load!

Just as a man who can carry
his own light with him,
is in far better situation...
than a another man who must depend on
another to light his way!

Your life will not change...
until you change the way
that you "spell" your life!

Ingested food is like ingested ideas
most of the time you
won't recognize them
when you are forced to release
them back into the world!

The most dangerous creature who ever lived
is the being who lets another
"think" for him!

For the important issues in life
one has the greatest counselor available...
the God spirit within!
To make matters clear...
How many of you need to be reminded by another
that you are thirsty...hungry...or in pain?
So it is with the affairs of the heart
seek thine own counsel from the God within!

Believing is seeing...
you always see what
you believe!

Separation does not exist...
all are a part of the One!

Like mentality attracts like reality
If your mental state tells you that you are cold...
you will shiver!
If your mental state tells you that you are hot...
you will sweat!
Your mental condition always creates your
present life reality!

Bridges are designed for one thing...
To transport one over a obstacle,
no matter how magnificent their design.
People, places, and conditions can be your bridges...
Look back over your life and witness the many bridges
you have crossed!

Discouragement is like apathy,
and apathy is like unto rain...
It touches all human form

Anxiety covets humanity
as Aroma to a rose,
both enter sweetly...
And eventually in time,
both find cause to sorrow
for yesterday's morn!

A fish out of water is like unto
a drunken man...
their destiny's are in the hand
of another
And both are lost!

Apples and peaches are as sweet to the palette
as rain is to an earthen worm

The tears from your Soul
are like unto
"manna" from Heaven...
Both celebrate the power
of God!

God is closer than
your last heartbeat
and your next
breath!

What mattereth a leaf on a tree...
when it's bretheren are beneath
it on the ground?
Who saith "survival" is not
lonely sometimes?

A whale sings to its mate
A dolphin to its calf
The water to its brook
and mankind to its folly!

Mankind has become drunk
from his pleasures
and is becoming numb
to spiritual intimacy...
for what pleasure brings a kiss...
without desire from its author?

A poor man
is only truly poor
when he is lost to all hope!

The cancer of hopelessness
is the true killer of mankind
*weapon of mass destruction

There is no friendship
in the darkness...
for they can't see each other,
All are blind
to the other's humanity!

God has enough martyrs
why don't you really
be brave...
and live for him?

Takes more courage
to love the one next to you
than cast a cold shoulder!

Face your neighbor
and let your hearts talk
before thine lips move!

When you do this
you will find out
that you are both only
extensions of the one God

You say
you really want to know me...

Here is a grand experiment...
Look deeply into a stranger's eyes
until you see me ...
It should take all of 1 second!

My blood quickens
and my heart races
when I ponder being
in the presence of my God

When I ask my Angels
to hold me and close my eyes...
sometimes I'm afraid
to open them
In case they're really there

How many want to really see God...
or really see Jesus?
be honest...be honest
If they really showed up
directly in front of you in full 3-D...
would you run and hide...faint...
or say "it was just your imagination"
and deny Him?

Humankind
We are funny creatures...
we long so hard
to be free of our mothers
and yet all through life
we keep longing for that
symbolic breast of comfort
where we feel safe!

We leave the womb and yet
for a lifetime
we make it our "Holy Grail"
until our body begins to decay...

How sad
when we finally figure out that we
are all grown up
and our egos won't fit!

It is said the sound of a human tear
shattering to the ground
is equal unto
Thunder rolling across our heavens
to our Guardian Angels listening...
How devastating our weeping
must be to our
Creation's God!

I anchor the Christ with my breath...
and I anchor God with my desire!

Here is God's elaborate plan for you...
"Follow your heart's desire!"
Do it now...
You will always have doubts
and you will always have
misgivings...
The key is to "Do it anyway!"

The hopeless are growing in voice,
the disheartened are growing in deed...
Woe to him who cannot recognize
the tear in his brother's eye!

Disappointment is like unto a man on fire
there is no relief until the flames are
extinguished and God's ointment of time
give easement to his injury!
Time covers us like a protective scab
and then disappears and makes us
forget it was even there!

The circumstances of everyday living
can seem like a box to a man
until Gods nudges man to open his
own gifts and find that the box
has no lid!

There are always choices in every
situation...however some may be more
desirable than the other...
Its akin to reaching into a box of
chocolates, if one does not satisfy your
tastes...then reach for another!

When a friend gives his word
you can stand on it!
When you can stand no longer
"on his hill..."
The heart may say
"ado!"

I once stood witness to a shining rock...
it did not move!
With my Human earthly eye
I perceived no movement.

With my Spiritual eye
I witnessed a theatre of
life within it!

And with my Soul's eye
I was shown how God
sometimes hides his
life from us

In my hearts secret place
I wondered why my human peace-of-mind
does not stay present to me
as the stillness stands
with its rock?

When mankind begins to attack
his children...
Armageddon
is not that far behind!

The mutilations of the innocents
brings about the gnashing
of teeth
As elders cry
"Save us from our seeds of youth!"

Some men are as dead
to their heart's feelings...
as a old penny that's
lying deeply buried in the grass...

Its of no value
until new eyes rediscover
it's worth!
and restore it's luster!

The worst villain
that I have ever encountered
stands before me in
my shaving mirror

The greatest hero
that I have ever encountered
daily holds the razor
to his own throat

What face of God
will you show your neighbor today...
stand you to empower or disempower
those you call to grace?

An echo is like unto
the voice of God...
it always keeps
repeating itself!
until it's stilled by the rocks of the human heart

Today I judged 10 men innocent
and 1 man guilty...
as I have judged, so be it unto me!
The condemned man hangs
himself by his own pen...
it was only myself
that I condemned this day!

My last thoughts for you

Know that regardless of age we are both teacher and student.

The uniqueness of each individual is how he/she expresses the knowledge they have been given, and how that will support and empower those brought into your awareness for their highest and best.

You were uniquely designed by God to succeed at accomplishing your particular purpose for being born on this earth during these current times...you showed up for a reason...Do you think your being born was an accident? Do you really believe God designed you by accident, kept you alive by accident, and that you are now reading these words... holding this book...holding these pages by accident?

Ding...Ding...Ding.... Wake up my beloved!

We are all simply here for God!

Are you right now doing your life's work? If not...why not? If not now...when?

You were divinely designed to do a particular work regardless of your present circumstances.

Ding...Ding...Ding... Time to "punch in" my beloved!

Higher Love & Light,
David Morris Jamison

Poetmanpeoria1@yahoo.com

www.ingramcontent.com/pod-product-compliance
Lightning Source LLC
Chambersburg PA
CBHW022013090426

42741CB00007B/1010